Our Family Tree

Family Name

_____

Date

_____

Great-Grandmother

Great-Grandmother

Great-Grandfather

Great-Grandfather

Grandmother

Grandfather

Father

Sisters & Brothers

Great-Grandmother

Great-Grandmother

Great-Grandfather

Great-Grandfather

Grandmother

Grandfather

Mother

Sisters & Brothers

Childr...

OUR FAMILY

A Keepsake Book

Written by Barbara Briggs Morrow

www.debbiemumm.com

new seasons®

Artwork © Debbie Mumm

Written by Barbara Briggs Morrow

New Seasons is a registered trademark of Publications International, Ltd.

Louis Weber, CEO
Publications International, Ltd.
7373 North Cicero Avenue
Lincolnwood, Illinois 60712

www.pilbooks.com

Permission is never granted for commercial purposes.

Manufactured in China.

8 7 6 5 4 3 2 1

ISBN-13: 978-1-4127-5910-6
ISBN-10:1-4127-5910-2

Contents

Introduction

Letters and journals, photo albums and scrapbooks are rare and invaluable links to the past. They are more precious still when written by your own grandparents, great-grandparents, or distant relatives. What were their stories, their hopes, and their passions? Who did they love?

Have you ever discovered a journal or a letter written by an ancestor that gave you new insight into your family's history? If so, you will know that the value of such records cannot be overestimated. If you never had the good fortune to know the history of your ancestors, this is your opportunity to begin a tradition. This keepsake book may be a lasting heirloom for your descendants, who will want to know about you and your family, your hopes, and your history.

Fill in the first chapter of the keepsake book so that your family will know all about your relatives and ancestors. You may then write your own story, using the chapters as a personal journal or a letter to your loved ones. Present the finished book to your children, so they will know their family intimately. The journal may be passed on to your grandchildren, and on through the generations. You are not only documenting a personal memoir; you are creating an invaluable heirloom for generations to come.

Genealogy Resources

Here are some useful genealogy resources to help get you started as you compile your family's unique history.

National Genealogical Society (NGS)

www.ngsgenealogy.org

The WorldGenWeb Project

www.worldgenweb.org

The USGenWeb Project

www.usgenweb.org

The Library of Congress

www.loc.gov

The U.S. National Archives and Records Administration

www.nara.gov

Tracing Our Roots

Think of this section as your family tree in sentence format,
giving generations to come the story of their origins.

All About Me

My full name is _____

This is the language from which our last name originates: _____

_____

In this language, our last name means _____

Our ancestors spelled and pronounced our last name like this _____

_____

I was born in this city and state _____

_____

My birthday is _____

I was born at this location _____

at this time _____

Here is a story that my parents told me about my birth _____

_____

_____

_____

_____

_____

Place photo Here

This is the story behind my name _____

_____

_____

My nickname is _____

It was given to me by _____

because _____

When I was growing up, this is how I felt about my nickname _____

_____

This is how I feel about my nickname today _____

_____

_____

Grand Beginnings

Place Photo of
Maternal Grandparents Here

My grandmother's full name is _____

She was born in this location _____

at this time _____

My grandmother is _____ generation American.

I called her _____

and this is the story behind the name _____

_____

_____

_____

_____

This is a special memory I have about my grandmother _____

_____

_____

_____

_____

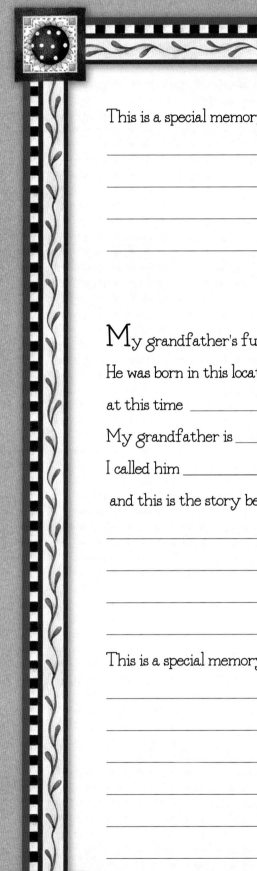

My grandfather's full name is _____

He was born in this location _____

at this time _____

My grandfather is _____ generation American.

I called him _____

and this is the story behind the name _____

_____

_____

_____

_____

This is a special memory I have about my grandfather _____

_____

_____

_____

_____

_____

_____

Place Photo of
Paternal Grandparents Here

My grandmother's full name is _____

She was born in this location _____

at this time _____

My grandmother is _____ generation American.

I called her _____

and this is the story behind the name _____

_____

_____

_____

_____

This is a special memory I have about my grandmother _____

_____

_____

_____

_____

My grandfather's full name is _____

He was born in this location _____

at this time _____

My grandfather is _____ generation American.

I called him _____

 and this is the story behind the name _____

_____

_____

_____

_____

This is a special memory I have about my grandfather _____

_____

_____

_____

_____

_____

My Parents

Place Photo of Parents Here

My mother's full name is _____

She was born in this location_____

at this time _____

My mother is _____ generation American.

This is a story my mother told me about her childhood _____

_____

_____

_____

_____

_____

This is the best advice my mother gave me _____
_____
_____

Here is what I admire most about my mother _____
_____
_____

My father's full name is _____

He was born in this location _____

at this time _____

My father is _____ generation American.

This is a story my father told me about his childhood _____
_____
_____
_____

This is the best advice my father gave me _____
_____
_____

Here is what I admire most about my father _____
_____
_____
_____

Brothers and Sisters

I am the _____ child.

I have _____ brothers and _____ sisters.

Their names and birthdays are _____

_____

_____

_____

_____

_____

_____

_____

These are the names and birthdays of their spouses and children _____

_____

_____

_____

_____

_____

_____

_____

_____

_____

When we were little, we would squabble about _____

_____

_____

_____

_____

This is the activity that I most enjoy sharing with my siblings _____

_____

_____

_____

_____

_____

_____

_____

_____

Some other special sibling memories are _____

_____

_____

_____

_____

_____

_____

My Other Half

My spouse's full name is_____

My spouse is named after _____

This is the story behind the name _____

My spouse's nickname is_____, but this is the pet name I use

_____

My spouse was born in this location _____

on this date _____ This is the story of our marriage proposal

_____

_____

_____

_____

_____

_____

_____

_____

_____

_____

_____

_____

_____

We were married at this location _____

_____

on this date_____

Here is a description of our wedding _____

_____

_____

_____

_____

_____

_____

This is where we spent our honeymoon _____

_____

Here is a description of the honeymoon _____

_____

_____

_____

_____

_____

My fondest memory of my first year of marriage is _____

_____

_____

_____

_____

_____

My Spouse's Parents

Place Photo of Parents Here

My mother-in-law's full name is _____

She was born in this location _____

_____

at this time _____

She is _____ generation American.

This is a story my mother-in-law tells about her childhood _____

_____

_____

_____

This is the best advice my mother-in-law gave us _____

_____

_____

Here is what we admire most about my mother-in-law _____

_____

_____

_____

My father-in-law's full name is _____

He was born in this location _____

at this time _____

He is _____ generation American.

This is a story my father-in-law tells about his childhood _____

_____

_____

This is the best advice my father-in-law gave us _____

_____

_____

Here is what we admire most about my father-in-law _____

_____

_____

_____

_____

My Spouse's Grandparents

Place Photo of
Maternal Grandparents Here

The full name of my spouse's grandmother is _____

She was born in this location _____

at this time _____

She is _____ generation American.

My spouse called her _____

and this is the story behind the name _____

_____

_____

_____

_____

Here is my spouse's favorite memory about this grandparent _____

_____

_____

_____

_____

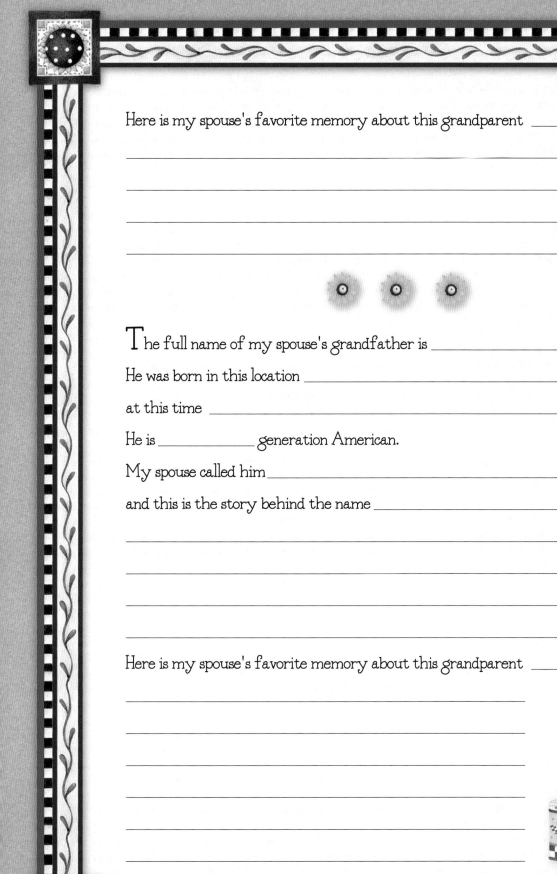

The full name of my spouse's grandfather is _____

He was born in this location _____

at this time _____

He is _____ generation American.

My spouse called him_____

and this is the story behind the name _____

_____

_____

_____

_____

Here is my spouse's favorite memory about this grandparent _____

_____

_____

_____

_____

_____

_____

Place Photo of
Maternal Grandparents Here

The full name of my spouse's grandmother is _____

She was born in this location _____

at this time _____

She is _____ generation American.

My spouse called her _____

and this is the story behind the name _____

_____

_____

_____

_____

Here is my spouse's favorite memory about this grandparent _____

_____

_____

_____

_____

The full name of my spouse's grandfather _____

He was born in this location _____

at this time _____

He is _____ generation American.

My spouse called him _____

 and this is the story behind the name _____

_____

_____

_____

_____

Here is my spouse's favorite memory about this grandparent _____

_____

_____

_____

_____

My Little Ones

My children's names and birthdays are _____

_____

_____

_____

_____

Here is a special memory about each of my children's births _____

_____

_____

_____

_____

_____

_____

This is the most rewarding part of being a parent _____

_____

_____

_____

The most challenging part about being a parent is _____

_____

_____

_____

_____

My Grandkids

My grandchildren's names and birthdays are _____

_____

_____

_____

_____

My grandchildren call me _____

This is the story behind the name _____

_____

_____

_____

_____

The most wonderful part of being a grandparent is _____

_____

_____

_____

_____

_____

_____

Place Photo Here

Through the Generations

This is a dominant family trait that every parent in my family hopes to pass on

_____

_____

_____

_____

_____

_____

People often think my children resemble me in these ways _____

_____

_____

_____

_____

_____

This is a dominant physical feature in my family _____

_____

_____

_____

_____

_____

_____

I am like my mother because _____

_____

_____

_____

_____

_____

_____

_____

_____

I am like my father because _____

_____

_____

_____

_____

_____

_____

_____

_____

CHILDHOOD STORIES

Here is a place to record special childhood memories and
provide a quick glance at the world in which you grew up.

Home

I grew up in _____

and lived there for _____ years.

Here is a description of my house and yard _____

_____

_____

_____

_____

This is what my childhood bedroom looked like _____

_____

_____

_____

Here is a description of the neighborhood where I grew up_____

_____

_____

These are the shops and restaurants I loved to visit when I was little _____

_____

_____

_____

My Friends

My best friend growing up was _____

Here is the story of how we met _____

_____

_____

_____

We most enjoyed playing these games _____

_____

When I was growing up, the most popular game to play with friends was _____

_____

I am still in touch with these childhood friends _____

_____

Here is a story my friends like to tell about me _____

_____

_____

_____

_____

_____

_____

_____

_____

_____

Our Pets

These are the pets I had growing up _____

_____

Here are the stories behind my pets' names _____

_____

_____

The funniest story I remember about one of my pets is _____

_____

_____

_____

As a child, I had these responsibilities when it came to our family pets _____

_____

Here is what I enjoyed doing with my pets _____

_____

_____

_____

_____

Entertaining Moments

My parents played these records _____
_____
_____

My family and I watched these television shows _____
_____

and listened to these radio programs _____
_____

My favorite bedtime story was _____

It was about _____
_____
_____

This was the most popular movie when I was a child _____

The top movie stars back then were _____

It cost _____ to go to the movies.

When I was a child, this is what my family and I did for fun ____
_____
_____
_____
_____
_____
_____
_____

Political Point of View

When I was born, the president was _____

The country's top concerns were _____

_____

These were all the presidents who served during my lifetime _____

_____

_____

This is one significant international or national event that I remember from

my childhood _____

_____

_____

When I heard the news, I was _____

_____

_____

I lived through this war when I was a child _____

_____

This is how the country's involvement in this war shaped my life

_____

_____

_____

_____

_____

To Be a Kid Again

This is my earliest memory _____

_____

_____

_____

My fondest childhood memory is _____

_____

_____

_____

If I could relive one event during my childhood, it would be _____

_____

_____

This is how we dressed when I was a kid _____

_____

I received _____ for allowance as a child.

I spent my money on _____

_____

As a child, my hero was _____

I looked up to this person because _____

_____

_____

_____

_____

The Teen Scene

Every generation of teens has a nickname, like Bobby-soxers and Generation X.

The nickname for my generation was _____

Here's a description of me as a teenager _____

_____

_____

_____

_____

_____

This is how I felt about the way I looked _____

_____

_____

I started dating when I was _____ years old.

Here is a description of a typical date _____

_____

_____

_____

_____

_____

_____

_____

My curfew was _____

This is the story of the first time I fell in love _____

_____

_____

_____

_____

_____

I spent my money on _____

_____

_____

_____

My favorite bands and entertainers were _____

_____

_____

I did / did not see this person or band perform live _____

_____

When I was a teenager, these were the popular places to hang out _____

_____

_____

_____

Here are some of the phrases that teenagers used when I was growing up _____

_____

_____

_____

School Days

As this section proves, education is so much
more than reading, writing, and arithmetic!

ABC's

The name of my elementary school was _____

It had _____ grades and _____ students.

This is how I got to school each morning _____

_____

This is how children were disciplined when I was in grade school _____

_____

_____

My favorite elementary school teacher was _____

This teacher was special because_____

_____

_____

_____

_____

_____

_____

_____

My favorite subjects in elementary school were _____

_____

_____

_____

My least favorite subjects were _____

_____

_____

_____

I was this type of student in elementary school _____

_____

_____

Here is a description of how I dressed in school _____

_____

_____

_____

I started to get homework in this grade _____

My favorite games at recess were _____

_____

_____

_____

_____

_____

Beyond classroom studies, these were the school activities that I most enjoyed _____

_____

_____

_____

_____

When I was in school, we did / did not have physical education. These were the games

we participated in _____

_____

_____

_____

When I was in school, we did / did not have music and art education.

This was my favorite creative activity _____

_____

_____

_____

_____

Here is a description of lunchtime at my school_____

_____

_____

_____

_____

_____

_____

Reaching Higher

This was the name of my high school _____

There were _____ students in my graduating class.

I got to school each day by _____

The high school teacher who most influenced me was _____

_____

because _____

_____

_____

My favorite subjects in high school were _____

_____

_____

_____

_____

_____

_____

My least favorite subjects were _____

_____

_____

I was this type of student _____

_____

_____

When I was in high school, I had to take these classes that are no longer mandatory today (like Home Economics or Shop) _____

_____

In these classes, I learned _____

_____

_____

_____

This is how I normally dressed for school _____

_____

I did / did not participate in high school sports.

These were my favorite sports _____

_____

Beyond classroom studies, I was involved in these school activities _____

_____

_____

I normally ate lunch with _____ and we talked about

_____

I did / did not attend my high school prom. The prom's theme song was _____

_____

Here is a description of a school dance _____

_____

_____

_____

_____

Ivy~Covered Walls

I attended this college _____

for these years _____

I chose to attend this college because _____

_____

_____

_____

Tuition was _____

My family paid for tuition by _____

_____

_____

Here is a description of the campus _____

_____

_____

_____

_____

_____

_____

_____

_____

_____

_____

My major was _____

I selected this major because _____

_____

_____

The professor that most influenced my life decisions was _____

This professor influenced me because _____

_____

_____

_____

The one class that really opened my eyes and set the wheels in motion toward bigger

things was _____

because _____

_____

_____

_____

_____

_____

_____

_____

_____

_____

I did / did not live in the dormitory. Here is a description of my living arrangements

_____

_____

_____

_____

My first roommate was _____

_____

Beyond classroom studies, I participated in these activities _____

_____

_____

_____

This is what my friends and I did for fun _____

_____

_____

_____

Looking back, the best part of my college days was _____

_____

_____

_____

_____

_____

_____

Family Holidays

Here is a place to pass on wonderful family traditions associated with the holidays.
Be generous with details and include recipes when you can!

Our Traditions

These are the holidays that we celebrate with a big dinner every year _____
_____
_____

We usually share these dinners with _____
_____
_____
_____

We always serve _____
_____
_____
_____

This is my favorite holiday memory _____
_____
_____
_____
_____
_____
_____

Wonderful Wintertime Holidays

This is the wintertime holiday that my family looks forward to _____

_____

_____

_____

_____

We share this holiday with _____

 on this day _____

_____

_____

_____

_____

My favorite childhood memory or story about this holiday is _____

_____

_____

_____

_____

_____

_____

_____

The oldest family tradition associated with this holiday is _____

_____

_____

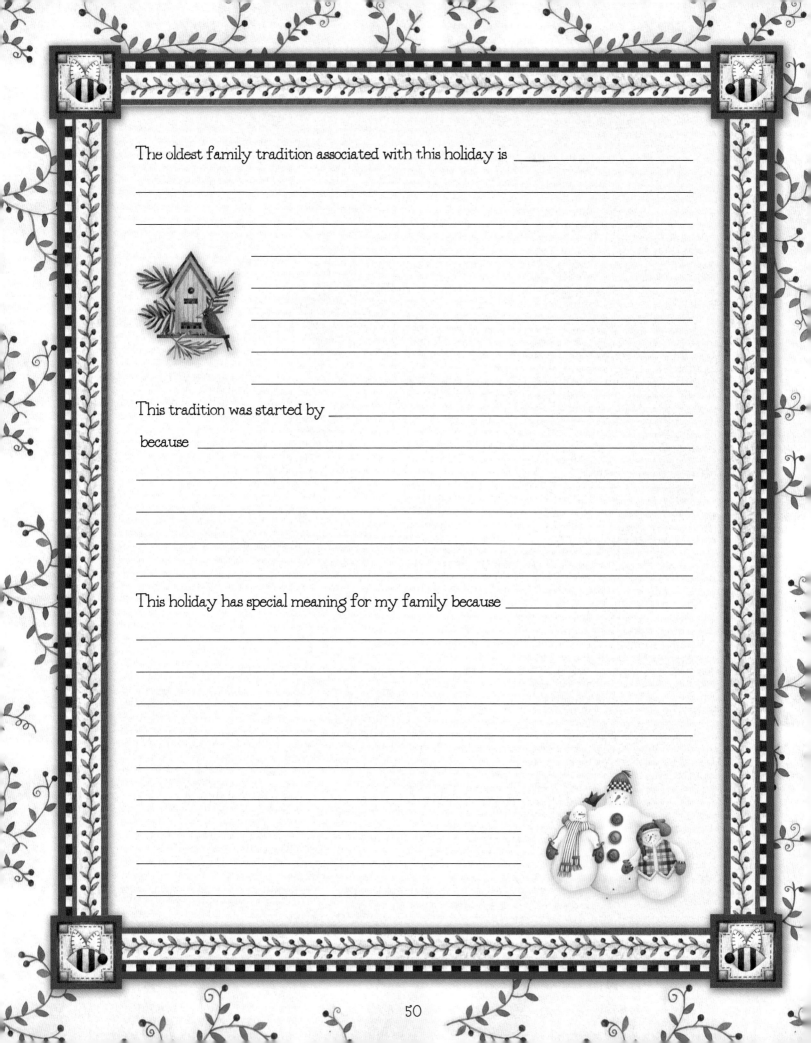   _____

_____

_____

_____

_____

This tradition was started by _____

because _____

_____

_____

_____

_____

This holiday has special meaning for my family because _____

_____

_____

_____

_____

_____

_____

_____

_____

This is what the adults most enjoy about this holiday _____

_____

_____

_____

This is what the kids most enjoy about this holiday _____

_____

_____

_____

_____

These are our traditions when it comes to giving gifts _____

_____

_____

_____

_____

This is what the gifts were like when I was young _____

_____

_____

_____

_____

This is how gift-giving has changed over time _____

_____

_____

_____

Another holiday that is important to my family is _____
_____
_____

These family members traditionally gather for this holiday _____
_____
_____
_____
_____
_____

We celebrate at this location _____
_____
_____

A favorite childhood memory or story about this holiday is _____
_____
_____
_____
_____
_____
_____
_____
_____
_____
_____

When it comes to this holiday, the traditions that I most want to pass along to the next generation are _____

_____

_____

_____

_____

_____

This is the special food that I associate with this holiday _____

_____

_____

_____

Here is the recipe for my favorite holiday dish _____

_____

_____

_____

_____

_____

_____

_____

_____

_____

_____

Traditions and Folklore

Many cherished traditions and tales are unique to your family,
like preserving an heirloom christening gown or performing birthday
customs. Here is a place for you to note all of it for future generations.

Vacation Memories

This is what family vacations were like when I was a child _____

_____

_____

_____

While growing up, my family returned to this particular vacation spot again and again

_____

_____

My most special memory of this place is _____

_____

_____

_____

_____

_____

_____

_____

_____

My favorite vacation I took with my own family is _____

_____

_____

_____

_____

_____

_____

My most special memory of this trip is _____

_____

_____

_____

_____

_____

_____

_____

This is a vacation-related tale that my family loves to tell _____

_____

_____

_____

_____

_____

_____

Summer Fun

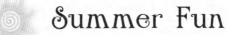

School's out! As a child, this is what I did for fun during the summer _____

_____

_____

_____

_____

_____

_____

_____

_____

_____

This is the biggest difference between summertime for kids today compared to my

childhood _____

_____

_____

_____

_____

_____

_____

_____

_____

I went to this camp as a child _____

_____

It was located in _____

_____

I attended this camp for _____ years

Here is a camp story I shared with my children _____

_____

_____

_____

_____

_____

_____

_____

_____

_____

_____

_____

_____

_____

_____

_____

Family Reconnections

My family comes together every _____ for a reunion.

It is traditionally held _____

_____

These are the family members who usually attend _____

_____

_____

_____

The person who travels farthest to attend is _____

who comes all the way from _____

_____

I most look forward to this part of the reunion _____

_____

_____

_____

This is a story about my family that never gets old _____

_____

_____

_____

_____

_____

_____

The most emotional family reunion was _____

_____

_____

_____

_____

_____

_____

Food is a huge part of family reunions. Here is a description of a typical spread

_____

_____

_____

_____

_____

_____

The treat I most look forward to is_____

It's made by _____

A traditional game, activity, or competition that we have at family reunions is

_____

_____

_____

The winner of this event usually is _____

_____

Happy Birthday to You!

My family celebrates birthdays with this special tradition _____

_____

_____

_____

_____

_____

When I was a child, this is what birthday parties were like _____

_____

_____

_____

_____

_____

_____

_____

My children's or grandchildren's parties are different because _____

_____

_____

_____

_____

_____

_____

One particular birthday celebration that stands out in my memory is _____

_____

_____

_____

_____

My most memorable birthday gift as a child was _____

_____

This person usually bakes the birthday cakes for our parties _____

_____

This is a special birthday cake recipe that we use in our family _____

_____

_____

_____

_____

_____

_____

_____

_____

_____

Weekly Wonders

These were some weekly family traditions my family had when I was growing up

_____

_____

_____

_____

_____

_____

_____

_____

This is my fondest memory of this event _____

_____

_____

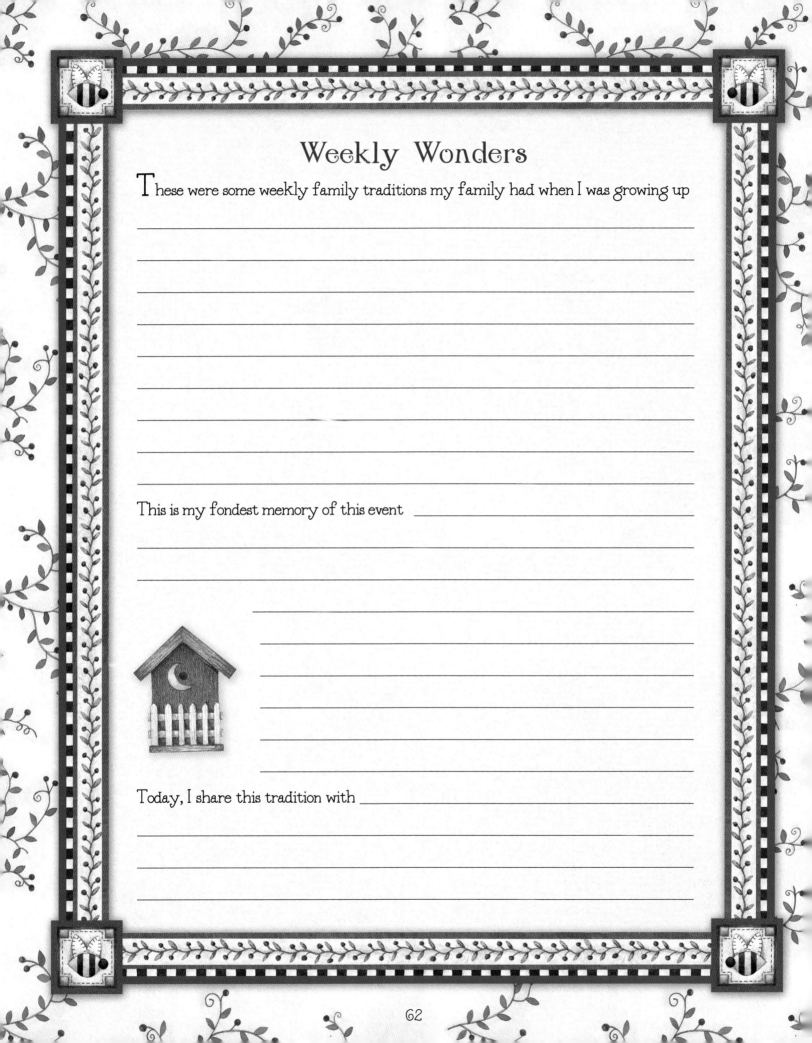

_____

_____

_____

_____

Today, I share this tradition with _____

_____

_____

_____

Spiritual Richness

I am this religion _____

_____

It is / is not the same religion I grew up with.

This is how important religion was in my childhood home _____

_____

_____

This is how important religion is in my home _____

_____

_____

I did / did not raise my children with this religion.

When there is marriage in our family, these religious traditions are honored _____

_____

_____

When a baby is born in my family, these religious ceremonies are performed _____

_____

_____

Here is a story connected to this event _____

_____

_____

_____

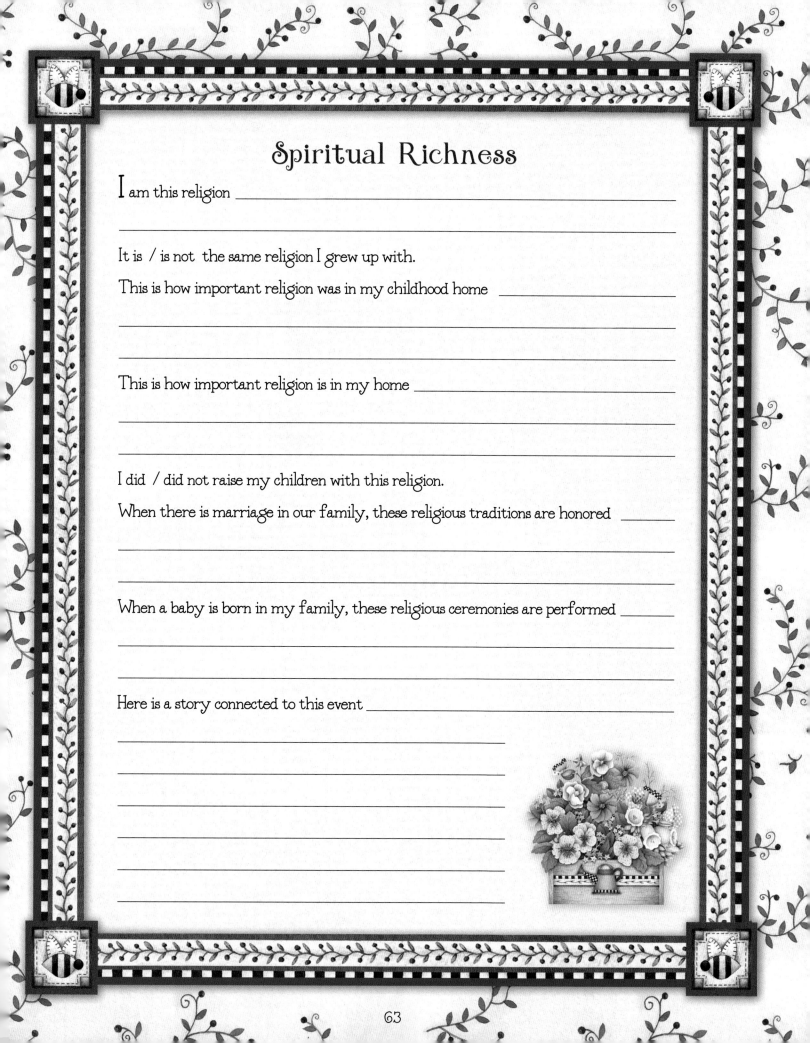

_____

_____

And the Title Goes To...

According to family reputation, tradition, and, of course, legendary folklore, assign a family member's name to each of the following titles. Remember...this is all good fun!!

Advice columnist in waiting _____

Animal fan _____

Artist _____

Blue~ribbon baker _____

Cuddle expert _____

Diva _____

Drama king or queen _____

Favorite photographer _____

First~place athlete _____

Friend to all _____

Gold~medal cook _____

Green thumb _____

Honorary beauty pageant winner _____

Inventive genius _____

Knee~slappin' comic _____

Legendary storyteller _____

Most creative mind _____

Penny~pincher _____

Political activist _____

Prankster _____

Problem solver _____

White~glove housekeeper _____

Wild child (age is irrelevant) _____

Tall Tales, Big Laughs

This is my favorite family story _____

_____

_____

_____

_____

_____

This is a story that my children enjoy repeating... much to my chagrin _____

_____

_____

_____

_____

_____

This is a story that I like to tell about my children... much to their dismay _____

_____

_____

_____

_____

_____

_____

9 TO 5 AND BEYOND

Give future generations a flavor for past work environments,
be it corporate or military — by filling in this section.

It's a Family Affair

Here is a description of the family-owned business that adult children in my family

naturally went into _____

_____

_____

_____

I did / did not go into the business. My children will / will not go into this family business.
This is how my children feel about their professional heritage _____

_____

_____

_____

Here are a few details about the history of this family business — how it began and
how it changed over the years _____

_____

_____

_____

_____

This is what my father did for a living _____
_____
_____

Here is how I felt about his career _____
_____
_____
_____
_____
_____

This is how my father dressed to go to work each morning _____
_____
_____
_____

My father gave me this advice about selecting a career _____
_____
_____
_____
_____
_____
_____
_____
_____

My mother did / did not have a career outside of the home. Here is a description of her

work _____

_____

_____

_____

_____

These were the career choices that were available to women when I was growing up

_____

_____

_____

_____

These were the career choices that were available to women when I was a young

adult _____

_____

_____

_____

_____

_____

_____

_____

_____

This is a woman in my family history who bucked tradition and went on to achieve

great things _____

Here is a description of what she did _____

_____

_____

_____

_____

_____

_____

She faced these roadblocks while pursuing her career _____

_____

_____

_____

_____

_____

Here is the advice my mother gave me on the subject of choosing a career _____

_____

_____

_____

_____

_____

_____

Pocket Change

My first after-school job was _____

_____ when I was _____ years old.

A typical job for people my age was _____

_____

My pay was _____ This was / was not a good rate at the time.

I used my paycheck for _____

_____

_____

_____

_____

_____

_____

Other jobs I had were _____

_____

_____

_____

_____

_____

_____

_____

The Corporate Ladder

My first career-related position was _____

_____

I began my career when _____

_____

Here is a description of my career path _____

_____

_____

_____

_____

_____

When I first started working, this is what corporate life was like _____

_____

_____

_____

_____

_____

Here is how things have changed in the corporate world since my first job _____

_____

_____

_____

_____

Uncle Sam

These people in our family pursued a military career _____
_____
_____

Here is a description of their military service _____
_____
_____
_____
_____
_____
_____
_____
_____

This is the advice I would give my child or grandchild about joining the military
_____
_____
_____
_____
_____
_____

When I was a young adult, this was the country's attitude toward the military system

_____

_____

_____

_____

_____

_____

_____

_____

_____

Here is how attitudes have changed _____

_____

_____

_____

_____

_____

_____

_____

_____

Our Medical History

Heredity is linked to many diseases and conditions. Today, medical technology can often prevent these conditions from developing — especially if your family has a medical tree.

Note any family members who had the following diseases or conditions. Include significant dates, such as approximate date of diagnosis and how old the person was when diagnosed. Also include any known medical reason for the disease or condition.

Allergies, including asthma _____

Alzheimer's disease _____

Cancer (specify type) _____

Cystic fibrosis _____

Depression, anxiety, or other psychiatric illness _____

Diabetes _____

Eye diseases _____

Hearing loss _____

Heart diseases _____

High blood pressure _____

Huntington's disease _____

Learning disabilities or mental retardation _____

Parkinson's disease _____

Polycystic kidney disease (PKD) _____

Reproductive conditions _____

Sickle cell anemia _____

Other _____

_____

SPECIAL NOTES

This is one piece of advice I would like to pass on to future generations _____

_____

_____

_____

This is something I would like to say to my children _____

_____

_____

_____

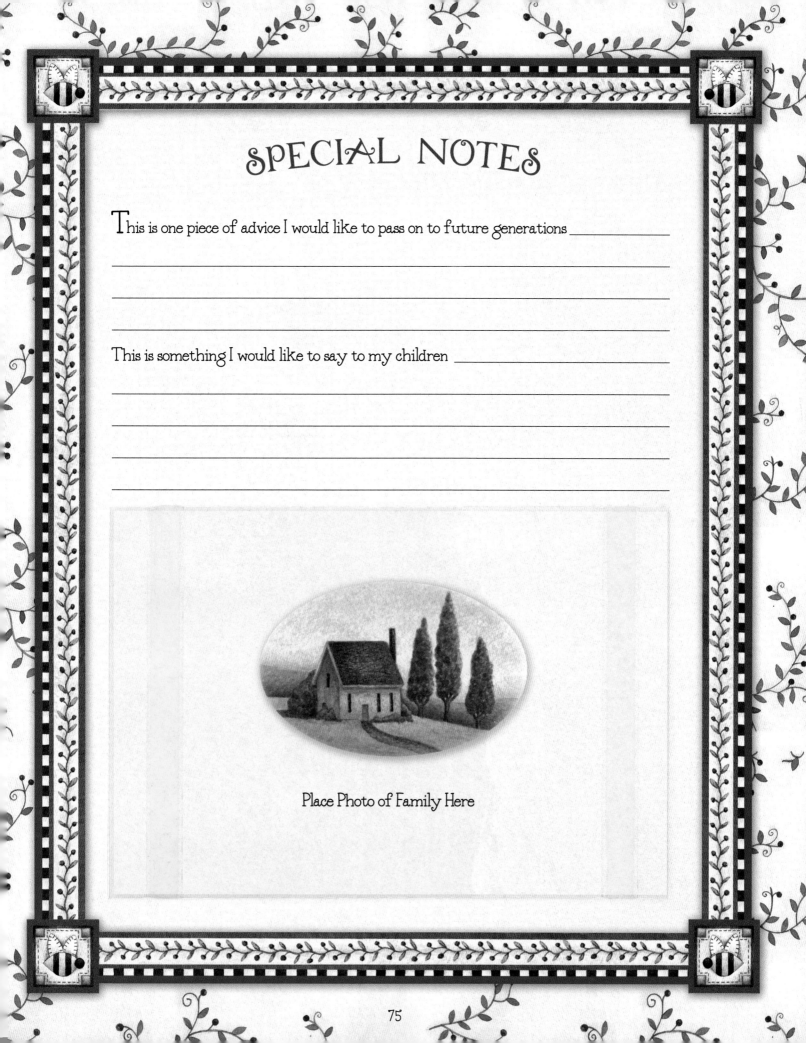

Place Photo of Family Here